My Dear Sister,
Thank you for sharing
your gifts and Talent
making this all
To God be the Glory!

Gaining Wealth

GOD'S Way

REVISED EDITION

Nicole Ford and Erica Russell

WESTBOW
PRESS®
A DIVISION OF THOMAS NELSON
& ZONDERVAN

WestBow Press
A Division of Thomas Nelson & Zondervan
1663 Liberty Drive
Bloomington, IN 47403
www.westbowpress.com
1 (866) 928-1240

ISBN: 978-1-9736-6614-1 (sc)
ISBN: 978-1-9736-6615-8 (e)

Print information available on the last page.

WestBow Press rev. date: 7/11/2019

CONTENTS

ACKNOWLEDGEMENTS

This book would not exist without the wisdom, knowledge, and help of some very special people. First, I would like to thank my Lord and Savior Jesus Christ and dedicate this book back to Him.

Secondly, I would like to thank Tytianna and Naomi for inspiring me on a daily basis. These two individuals continuously push me to become a better Christian.

I am delighted to acknowledge my grandmother Carrie Octavia Ford who was called home on November 19, 2001. It was her fervent prayers, firmness, and her wise counsel that helped me along the path. Thank you, God, for giving her the strength to take my siblings and I in and rear us to become mighty men and women of God. Witnessing her profound work ethic in kingdom building and the way she evangelized to the lost and brokenhearted made me understand my true purpose.

I would like to give special thanks to the amazing Pastor Edward J. Tyson (New Hope Baptist Church in Oklahoma City) for his continual words of encouragement, teaching, leadership, guidance, honesty, and prayers. His friendship is more precious than gold.

Bishop Tony Miller (The Gate Church in Oklahoma City), you are one of the best bible teachers I know. You have a zeal for the Lord and a way with words. You easily make being a Christian fun and attractive. You have shown me that God can take anyone above and beyond.

Saulie M. Tucker is one of the greatest mentors in my life. She has been boldly spreading the gospel since I have been a tween. You have been a vessel for decades and you're always allowing the Lord to fill you to be used for His Kingdom. Thank you for having my back one hundred percent and helping me care for what I cherish.

Thank you to the financial experts, who allowed me to interview them and pick their brains. Another special thanks to my astonishing family, the loves of my life, for their spiritual and moral teachings. I receive strength from the laughter, the warm hugs, and the kisses. Oh what precious memories!

Lastly, I gratefully acknowledge the marvelous spirit-filled editors and illustrator of this book. Mrs. Kathleen Smith, is an outstanding retired teacher in the Yukon, Oklahoma area; thanks for keeping me on the straight and narrow. Mrs. Kayleen Browning, another outstanding teacher for the Yukon School District; thanks for having such a gentle spirit. With deep appreciation I would like to thank the illustrator of this book, Mrs. Sharon Motley, I was able to give her my ideas and she allowed the Holy Spirit to lead her in creating masterpieces. Sharon has the sweetest smile and I take pride in calling her my friend.

May this book inspire single parents and grandparents who are rearing children without the help of a spouse or a support group. Never give up on your children.

When you meet God, your life is never the same. Please get ready for God to change your life. Know that if you keep God first in your life, every need shall be supplied.

INTRODUCTION

Today it seems as if no one is exempt from experiencing financial problems. From the government to a family of three residing in an urban community, why is it so difficult to control our finances? My friends, let's uncover together some conscious and unconscious behavioral patterns that can keep us from financial freedom. You will be set free and obtain the financial freedom that the Lord long to give. Thank the Lord financial freedom is attainable through knowledge, wisdom, obedience and discipline.

Throughout the years, I have often wondered why I couldn't get ahead financially. Being reared by my grandmother, a missionary who was a firm believer in tithing, giving alms, and sacrificial offerings, gave me an opportunity to learn valuable lessons on doing things **God's way** and according to His will. In fact, today I can still hear my grandmother's pleasant voice telling me to give my tithes and always to put the Lord first.

The Greek word for *tithe* is *apodekatoo* meaning "a payment, giving, or receiving a tenth of any property or produce (Tyndale et al., 2005)." Abram gave us an example of tithing before the Law of Moses was established.

> "And blessed be the most high God, which hath delivered thine enemies into thy hand.

And he gave him tithes of all." – Genesis
14:20 (KJV).

This passage takes us back to the time when Lot, Abram's nephew, was captured. The inhabitants of Sodom and Gomorrah (became prisoners of war), along with all their possessions we're taken captive by King Chedorlaomer and his allies. One man escaped captivity and reported the news to Abram (also known as Abraham and recognized for his great faith). Soon after, Abram gathered up 318 trained servants, armed them, and prepared them for battle. With help from God, Abram and his men (small in numbers) were victorious in bringing back Lot son of Haran, the inhabitants, and their possessions. The first war mentioned in scriptures was won by using the surprise and attack strategy. Restoration took place. Thereafter, Abram gave King Melchizedek (the first king/ priest of Scripture Heb.7:1 KJV) a tenth of the possessions. In Genesis 13 and 14, we discover two character traits about Abram. His faith had made him unselfish and bold.

A tenth is an ordinate number that may appear to be small, but this amount can be painful when offered to God begrudgingly. We are asked to leave a state of withholding and make a sacred unselfish sacrifice.

After witnessing what Christ can do, I have learned that when I cheerfully tithe first from my income, Christ honors my act of giving and takes care of my needs. It's good to tithe, but it is even better when you're elated by following God's instructions and your heart is right with God.

Sources:
Life Application Study Bible. Tyndale House Publishers, Inc., 2005
http://www.biblestudytools.com.,Thayer and Smith. "Greek Lexicon entry for Apodekatoo". "The NAS New Testament Greek Lexicon". . 1999.

CROSSOVER

I t hurt me deeply when a loved one, dear to me, stricken with cancer confessed, "I don't know if I am a Christian or where I would go if my journey would end on earth today." Although she sometimes went to church, at that very moment it was obvious a true relationship with God Almighty was missing from her life (seldom people know what its like to be a part of a church, but not a part of God's Kingdom). If we're truly honest with ourselves, most of us would be found guilty of trying to clad a void in our lives. First and foremost, allow God to fill the void in your life. If not, you will find yourself spending a large amount of time chasing after everything else and still feel emptiness. God is the only source that will not leave you empty. We assume that we have all the time in the world to invite God into our lives, but we may not. I urge you not to wait.

I have heard so many people say, "I wish that I knew the Lord before I became gravely ill." How many of you have heard a loved one or a friend make this statement, " I wished <u>so and so</u> would have accepted Christ as his/her Savior before he/she passed away."

What you are about to read will not make sense if God has not been given complete control of your life. You have to reposition yourself to reap the harvest. He has to become your Lord. I was able to share The *Plan of Salvation* with my loved one that day. She accepted Christ as her personal Savior, and that day the angels rejoiced in heaven because one soul was saved.

We must not only position people to begin life, but begin to equip people to transition in life as well. If it is difficult for you to establish a relationship with the Lord Jesus Christ, remove the obstacle of disbelief from your path and begin exercising your faith. The knowledge of knowing God and believing in Jesus Christ is the first step you must take to Salvation.

Maybe you are feeling as if you've done so many bad acts and your sins cannot be forgiven. You are not alone; others have felt this exact way before. The Good News is, your sins have already been forgiven. Jesus redeemed us more than 2000 years ago. He knew we would need a Savior, to save us from being slaves to sin. You must believe this report. Now it is time for you to accept this knowledge. God has a Word for you. Don't feel ashamed or if you have let Him down? The Lord has a word just for you today.

There is one God, eternally existing as the Trinity. Do you believe in God the Father, The Son (Jesus), and The Holy Spirit? God the Father is the creator of Heaven and Earth. The Son of God is He who died for our sins and rose from the dead so that we might be saved. Christ sent the Holy Spirit after He ascended to Heaven, to abide in us and guide us into all truth. The Spirit is the greatest search engine, searching facts known and unknown. These three are equal and shall be forever honored.

Before we go any further let us reposition ourselves and get to know our Sovereign God and Lord and Savior. Please open your heart and allow the Word of God to be planted and manifested. Join with me and believe.

St. John 3:16(KJV)
For God so loved the world, that he gave his only begotten Son, that whosoever believeth in Him should not perish, but have everlasting life.

Romans 3:10 (KJV)
As it is written, There is none righteous, no, not one.

Romans 3:23 (KJV)
For all have sinned, and come short of the glory of God.

Romans 5:8(KJV)
But God commendeth His love toward us, in that, while we were yet sinners, Christ died for us.

Romans 6:23 (KJV)
For the wages of sin is death; but the gift of God is eternal life through Jesus Christ our Lord.

Romans 10:9 (KJV)
That if thou shalt confess with thy mouth the Lord Jesus, and shalt believe in thine heart that God hath raised Him from the dead thou shalt be saved.

Romans 10:13 (KJV)
For whosoever shall call upon the name of the Lord shall be saved.

1 John 1:9 (KJV)
If we confess our sins, he is faithful and just to forgive us our sins, and to cleanse us from all unrighteousness.

Sources: Plan of Salvation*

CHAPTER 1

Putting God First

> Instead, be concerned above everything else
> with the Kingdom of God and with what he
> requires of you, and he will provide you with
> all these other things. Matthew 6:33 (GNT)

A t one point I grew tired of living from paycheck to
paycheck although God continued to provide for me.
I am a firm believer that God gives us the wisdom and
knowledge to help us live life more abundantly. These beliefs
led me to reevaluate my lifestyle, my relationship with God,
and take a closer look at some of the financial decisions I was
making.

After thorough evaluation, I pinpointed several errors.
First, God was not made top priority in my life (I gave Him
time when I wanted to give Him time. And, when I did spend
time with God, it was minimal.) . Second, I did not give God
totally access to every area in my life (there were areas in
my life that I had restricted the Holy Spirit from entering).
Truthfully speaking there were some negative behaviors
and sins that I did not want God to take away. My lifestyle
was customized so sinful behavioral would have a place.

Third, I looked at God only as a transitional God and not a transformational God. I wanted him to do things for me without changing my life. How many can attest to this form of thinking? I was always asking God to do something for me. His reputation was based on what He had done for me and not who He was.

The bible is filled with different principles. The above principle could be interpreted like this: *"See that His will be done first; turn to God for help first; fill your thoughts with His desires first; apply what His Word says regarding the situation first. Then He will provide you with peace, joy, good health, and with the other things that you seek."*

What is keeping you from putting God first? As a young adult, I trusted in everything the Creator created, but not Him. I trusted in men, my job, and the list went on and on. I was guilty of jumping into financial obligations without consulting God or fully preparing myself, lack of self-control (such as impulsive spending, excessive gambling) and being an enabler.

I had to distinguish the difference between a giver and an enabler. I enabled family members to persist in self-destructive behaviors by bailing them out of financial problems instead of being held accountable.

Not only was I facing these issues, but I also noticed my friends and colleagues were facing similar financial problems as well. I realized that I had strayed far away from my grandmother's financial teachings, and definitely far from God's principles. I had allowed my irresponsibility to form a stronghold in my life.

Instead of being concerned with what God had required from me, I was concerned about how people viewed me and with material possessions. I found myself in so much debt that I was screening my telephone calls.

"In the Old Testament the word *stronghold* was used to describe a fortress, but in the New Testament it is used to describe a prison." (Renner, 2003). I realized my carelessness had led me to prison.

After giving the Holy Spirit access, I begin listening and being obedient. Shortly after I begin applying the above principle to my life, I begin seeing a drastic change in each and every area in my life. My heart's desires changed. I begin wanting exactly what God wanted for my life. My prayers were being answered.

List Some Known Behavioral Patterns Causing You Financial Problems	

Trusting in the Lord

For some individuals, serving God is easy when life is going well, but what about when life seems as if it's falling apart? From a human perspective things were not getting better for me. My lack of obedience, self-control, and the inability to say no, were placing shackles on me one by one.

Like most young adults, sadly I thought that I could turn the situation around by myself, but quickly I came to find out that it was impossible. My debt slowly began to affect my attitude and my service to the building of God's Kingdom. In spite of what we go through, the duty of exemplification as Christians remains upon us.

As Christians, we must never allow human limitations to cause us to act out of character.

How is your obedience to God when circumstances are dangerous or unattractive? Do you spend more or less time with God during hardships? Do you only call out to God when you're in despair? Do you have a consistent relationship with God? Have you ever wondered, what if we did not have to worry about bills or what if problems did not exist? Would we ever come to know what God is capable of doing? Would we witness His power?

At this point, I had two options. I could wallow in my failures, or I could grab hold to God's grace and become an overcomer. Ironically, my financial crisis caused me to intertwine myself with God. I moved from wanting to please people to desperately wanting to please God. And not just with my time, spiritual gifts and talent, but with my finances also.

Briefly take a moment to put yourself in the shoes of Abram. Here is a man that in Genesis 12, God instructs him to leave the familiar to go into the unfamiliar. Not only does God tell Abram to go to a foreign land, God adds another 'shaker'. God tells Abram to leave his family and his community. I don't know about you, but I would have had a definite 'say what, say who' moment. I have heard that a faith that has not been tried or tested is a faith that cannot be trusted. You have to come to understand the way God dealt with Abram because that is the same way God deals with us sometimes. How many times has God told you to do something that absolutely does not make any sense to you at all at the moment? Your listening to God speak and you're left scratching your head ('say what, say who')? Your response may have went like this, "You want me to do what?" If you were text messaging, those words would be in all CAPS.

I have seen God turn the impossible to possible. There is nothing impossible for God. Simply put your trust in Him.

Establishing a Better Relationship
with God through Christ

The *Merriam-Webster's Dictionary* defines a *relationship* as the state of being connected, or a connection (1995). Are you living with an independent spirit? You keep telling yourself that you don't need anyone and you can make it on your own. Becoming connected with Christ is a choice that we make.

Although I was a Christian in my early twenties, my relationship with my Savior had grown cold. My heart had hardened. I found myself doing all the talking, and seldom listening. It was time for a change! The change had to start with my relationship with Christ. I needed the Spirit to stir up the fire within me. It was time for me to become spiritually fit. Some of us are physically fit (we eat, we workout, and we are in good shape), but spiritually anorexic (we lack spiritual substance. We don't feed ourselves the Word of God daily, we seldom pray, and we fail to be doers of the Word). Therefore, when the enemy comes to attack us, we are not prepared to fight. Some Christians tend to believe that since we are recipients of Grace, we do not have to do anything else. You have to understand, when you give your life to Christ, the enemy is upset. Any word that you plant in the soil of your heart the enemy is going to try to snatch it.

I was desperately seeking spiritual growth, so I headed back to bible study and began studying the Word. Thereafter, I found myself grasping a deeper understanding of God's Word, lining up my life with the Word, praying, meditating, learning how to use the spiritual weapons, and listening to God more each day. Suddenly, I had developed a fearsome thirst. I desired and needed to give my Savior more of me. I was determined to put Christ in the core of my personal life, my career, my business, my finances, and everything else that I was involved in. I gave Him full access. Christ is a gentleman. He is standing at the door of your heart knocking. You have to invite Him inside. He is not going to kick down the door. Will you allow Him to enter?

Are the storms of life blocking your reception, and interfering with your connection with God? Your relationship with Christ is the most valuable and free treasure in your life. Everyone is God's creation, but not everyone has chosen to be His child.

> O God, you are my God, and I long for you. My whole being desires you; like a dry, worn-out, and waterless land, my soul is thirsty for you. Psalm 63:1 (GNT)

The scripture above is part of what I consider a love letter that David had written. These words immediately come after Psalm 62, the message of hope. In this passage, David comes to identify God as Sovereign and in control. David places all of his trust in his God and urges us to as well. David doesn't stop writing this passage, until he gives us vital instructions. The writer persuades us to trust in God by listing some of His attributes (strong, dependable, and loving). David tells us not to put our trust in people and not to put our trust in riches.

"Establishing an intimate relationship with God is the key!"

What qualified King David to advised us on trust and an intimate relationship with God? A shepherd, who wasn't even recognized by his own father when Samuel was sent to them (Samuel 16 KJV). The bible records his many failures. His profile lists him as a betrayer, a liar, an adulterer and a murderer. Maybe that's why we can look at David as an expert, because despite all that he had been through his relationship with God, dependence on God, and love for God never ceased.

In Chapters 63, we find David running from someone. The mighty warrior and giant-killer is now alone in exile. This King has had his share of ups and downs. He was engulfed by envious people, jealous individuals, folks highly concerned about his position and how he got into position, people watching his every move and awaiting for his down fall. All of the hatred drove him to fear for his life and caused him to take flight. Some of us can relate to David. We are surrounded by negative Nancy's and people that will step on our necks to keep us from getting up, if we fall. These types of people frown when we're promoted and will lie on us as quick as lightening flashes.

In the midst of being alone, it gave David some time to reflect and remember the one and only friend that he could call on. After reflection and remembrance, he begins to express his love for God. David was deeply in love with God because He had shown him that He would be with him time after time. God is with you even when you are feeling alone or abandon my friends. In Chapter 62, the king list God's attributes, and in Chapter 63 David list his reaction to His goodness. It can be interpreted like this: God because you are strong, dependable, and loving; I earnestly seek you, my soul thirst for you, my body longs for you, my lips will glorify you, I will praise you, I will think of you, I will sing to you, and I will cling to you.

Satisfied with Jesus

Never did I imagine so much growth would come from my hardships. I speak as a woman of God; someone who has made it through the storms, deserts, and valleys.

"As believers, we must first allow our souls to prosper. The success as a child of the Most High, will always succeed any worldly success. If our soul is not well, prosperity is not inevitable. We must achieve an intimacy with Christ so strong that we cannot even fathom living without Him. You can accomplish anything the Lord sets out for you when you have a strong connection with Him." This is possible because you begin to walk in cadence with Him. We must passionately pursue Jesus and get to know Him. Let me reiterate, having knowledge of who Christ is, gives us the desire to please Him.

Do you thirst for the Lord? The Apostle Paul pursued an intimate relationship with Christ, which led him to giving Christ his all. Paul tells us to let nothing separate us from the love of God (Romans 8:35-39 KJV). Our intimacy compels us to go through our days talking with Christ, calling on His name, and surrendering to Him, all because He is everything to us.

I can remember when I first started dating. We couldn't go two hours without checking on each other. We wanted to talk on the telephone all night. I couldn't wait until the next morning just to hear the sound of that special voice, or listen to him breathe. In the same way, it's vital to form an even more intimate relationship with Christ. Our desires to be with Our Lord and Savior should be even more compelling.

Putting God First
Trusting in God **Getting to Know Him** **Being Satisfied with Him**

CHAPTER 2

Overcoming Hardships

My brethren, count it all joy when ye fall into
divers temptations; Knowing this, that the
trying of your faith worketh patience. But
let patience have her perfect work, that ye
may be perfect and entire, wanting nothing.
James 1:2-4(KJV)

It is a well-known fact Christians will experience hardships
and trials; however, do not allow times of trouble to
separate you from God. Our Lord wants us to see those
trying times as opportunities for refinements. God wants to
mature us. Do not allow your circumstances to overwhelm
you, consume you, or alter your attitude of thankfulness.
God will never give you a life were faith is not necessary. The
enemy is seeking to destroy your faith (Numbers 23:19; 1 John
5:4). The enemy wants to remove the belief that God will do
what He said He would do.

Have you responded to a situation such as sickness,
death, debt, divorce, loss of property, loss of employment,
incarceration, and contrary to your Christian character?
Sometimes the depth of our character is not revealed until

we are placed in an uncomfortable situation. Have you felt as if you're on a solitary journey and this feeling has disabled your praise? God has not abandoned you. If your human nature has caused you to act out of your Christian character seek forgiveness and repent. Our Father is merciful, but we must have a heart of repentance. I have learned that during our hardships we should be praying and reminding ourselves daily of God's promises. We must commit ourselves to our God and remain faithful.

Whatever was taken from you that left you in poverty, left you lacking, or left you spiritually dead can be restored. It is important for us to realize that we cannot do anything without the Master. Look in the mirror and tell yourself, "God plus me equals victory."

> Elimelech died, and Naomi was left alone with her two sons, who married Moabite women, Orpah and Ruth. About ten years later Mahlon and Chilion also died, and Naomi was left all alone, without her husband or sons. Ruth 1:3-5(GNT)

Here is a great example on faith, endurance, and dedication. Can you image moving to another state because your economy was so bad? Even your neighbors are stricken with poverty and without enough means to get by. Have you seen predicaments, where there were skilled and qualified people in a community, but a lack of job opportunities? You cannot go next door to ask for some water or flour, because they don't have neither necessities' either. Our problems serve a purpose.

This family can attest to this circumstance. The only solution to their famine problem was to move geographically.

There wasn't a problem with the family as a unit; it was the system or the economy that was broken. See most of the time when believers experience hardships such as this, they begin to look within and start to blame themselves.

Image having to leave your home and the people you care about the most leaves you. In this case, Naomi's family dies and there was no getting them back. She leaves her home with security and returns back home without the same security. Left as a widow in a harden-heart society. But, the book of James tells us of a way to profit from our trials. Your pain can be used as a stepping-stone toward faith. Then faith will change your environment.

Whenever you get a chance, read about Naomi's story in the book of Ruth. The story does not end on a bad note. Naomi and Ruth become prosperous and part of a royal lineage. This story will strengthen your soul.

Diving into the Word

A method to help us learn more about God and stand against adversities is studying the Word and hiding the Word of God in our hearts. The enemy will not cease an attacking us. Satan wants us to feel defeated before the fight even begins. When we are able to speak the Word against troubles and temptations, we will then witness snares and mountains being removed from our path. Diving into God's Word daily will give us courage and a peace of mind. The <u>Word of God</u> is the <u>Will of God</u>. The word '<u>will</u>' in Greek means '<u>thelema</u>', which is defined as <u>design, purpose, or plan</u>(Renner, 2003,pg.451).

The more intimate you become with Christ by studying the Holy Word and learning more about His earthly pilgrimage, the more you will begin to put your trust in Him and walk in His purpose. As you spend time meditating and reading the Word, your mind becomes renewed to God's way of thinking. When your mind is renewed, you become inwardly strengthen and difficult to deceived. The enemy knows that empty minds are much easier to deceive.

Keep in mind that lack of faith can be crippling. Wherefore, studying of scriptures increases our faith. Our willingness to study, know, and apply God's Word will have a direct effect on how God uses us. Do you feel as if you have let Him down too many times? Embrace the forgiveness of God and be grateful for what He has done for you. All of the answers to your questions, concerns, and prayers can be found in His Word. When we plant the Word of God in our hearts, keep it moist, and act accordingly, we will bear good fruit (Tyndale, 2005).

Speaking the Word

> The promises of the Lord can be trusted; they are as genuine as silver refined seven times in the furnace. Psalm 12:6(GNT)

We will not offend God by reminding Him of the works of His servant, and restating what He has promised us in His Holy Word. For example, if a predicament has left me fearful or discouraged, I say, "Master, this is Your servant who has tried her best to spread Your Word with my lips and life. Sometimes I miss the mark, but I have made up in my mind that I will continue to serve You. Master, Your Word says, *'Be strong and of a good courage; be not afraid, neither be thou dismayed: for the Lord thy God is with thee whithersoever thou goest.'* (Joshua 1:9 KJV)." As these words begin to come out of my mouth I am reassured that God will never lie to me or leave me. He will always keep His promise; therefore, I am no longer a slave to fear. You need to speak every word in faith knowing that it will produce great outcome. Faith has a focus and a desire.

After you begin studying God's word, the Holy Spirit will teach you which scriptures to apply to various attacks of the enemy. What ample assurance it is to know that we're in the Master's hand. You may have co-workers plotting to move you out of your position because of jealousy or hate, but when God stretches out His hand He will bring it to pass and nothing shall harm you. Please take a moment and say this prayer with me:

> Father, today I bind up all hindrances that have moved itself in the way of my prosperity. Lord, I am depending on you to turn this situation around. Lord, I declare that I am an overcomer. For you have taken bad situations and brought forth good outcomes before. Lord, I declare that I have the victory. I pray this in the mighty name of Jesus.

Taming the Tongue

> But the tongue can no man tame; it is an unruly evil, full of deadly poison.– James 3:8 (KJV)

According to Renner, the word *tame* comes from the Greek word *damadzo*, which means "to subdue, to have under control or restraint (Renner, 2003)." Our world is voice activated. I am a great stickler for positive affirmation and affirmative response. I strongly believe that God gave His sons and daughters power, and that same power can be loose by the tongue. When we pray for God to increase our income or financially bless us, we cannot speak about how "broke" we are. If we do, we display a lack of faith. The negative language spoken can cancel out the prayer. It is important to choose your diction wisely. "Most importantly, we must ask for God's Spirit to help us control our tongues. The tongue can only be tamed by the Spirit." (Renner, 2003).

> Suddenly a strong wind blew up, and the waves began to spill over into the boat, so that it was about to fill with water. Jesus stood up and commanded the wind, "Be quiet!" and he said to the waves, "Be still!" The wind died down, and there was a great calm. - Mark 4:37,39(GNT)

I know you're probably thinking that the wind and the waves obeyed the voice of Jesus because He is the Son of God. And, that is absolutely true! When Jesus says something it is good as done. But, that same power lives in us because His Spirit lives in us. Listen, Jesus would not instruct us to speak to a mountain and tell the mountain to move if we did not have power (Matthew 17:20 KJV). Jesus doesn't just say things to be saying them. Jesus knows what He put inside of us; so in the above supportive text He leads by example. Jesus shows us just how to use our power. Opening our mouths and speaking powerful words to our circumstances releases the power.

Please take note, Jesus and the disciples went through the storm at the end of chapter four, right before a miraculous healing takes place in chapter five. When Jesus heals a man with evil spirits. This is exactly how situations occur in our lives. We can be right on the edge of experiencing a breakthrough, when suddenly we encounter attacks from every side. This was not a small storm; this storm was so huge that water began filling the boat. When you look at the situation, you automatically infer and think they are about to drown. But, Jesus does something amazing. The bible says, He speaks twice. He speaks to the wind and then He speaks to the waves. He told both what He wanted or expected them to do. Both obeyed.

Meditation and Praise

> Finally, brethren, whatsoever things are true, whatsoever things are honest, whatsoever things are just, whatsoever things are pure, whatsoever things are lovely, whatsoever things are of good report; if there be any virtue, and if there be any praise, think on these things. Philippians 4:8 (KJV)

I have to admit, the above scripture is one of my favorites and has been since my teenage years. There was a song that our youth choir would sing with this scripture embedded. Of course, the song became one of my favorite songs. I can recite this scripture over and over again in my head. Guess what? I have many times. The Bible instructs us to set our minds on pure and lovely things because settled thoughts can become actions (Philippians 4:8). It's through meditation we are able to take our minds off the problem and set it on the power of God. I experience peace when meditating, and peace reconciles me with God. Meditation helps us bring circumstances back into a God's perceptive. We need to see situations the way God sees them, and God sees them as small. Either God ordains or allows situations to occur in our lives.

There are three natural responses to adversity: retreat, fight, and praise. Occasionally, as we face adversities, we immediately hit the panic button discrediting our God. I am here to tell you that desperation has a sound. Sometimes we can be in a condition so long that we get tired and desperate. You better open your mouth and praise God.

Through meditation we are led by the Holy Spirit to hit the praise button. Thinking of the goodness of the Lord brings forth praise! Your praise holds value because God desires your praise. It's your praise that acknowledges that God has authority and all power to turn the situation around. There are people watching Christians and paying attention to how we react to certain situations. Our best testimony is when they can witness Christians going through trials and tribulations with a song on our hearts and praise in our mouth. Our Sovereign Creator is capable of handling any situation, and giving us peace in the midst of trouble (Isaiah 26:3). If you will begin 15-20 minute meditations daily, you will experience spiritual growth, as well as a closer relationship with your Heavenly Father. Remember David in Psalm 63, he found nourishment in mediation and praise. David said, " I will praise you as long as I live, and in your name I will lift up my hands...with singing lips my mouth will praise you. On my bed I remember you; I think of you through the watches of the night."

Prayer

After consulting with the people, the king ordered some musicians to put on the robes they wore on sacred occasions and to march ahead of the army, singing: "Praise the Lord! His love is eternal!" When they began to sing, the Lord threw the invading army into a panic. 2 Chronicles 20:21;22 (GNT)

Nicole Ford and Erica Russell

I know you maybe wondering what does this text have to do with prayer. As believers, it is important for you to understand how prayer can be utilized as an offensive and defensive strategy. This text helps us see how fully equipped we are and how to used each and every weapon against the enemy. Get ready to take notes. Let's dive into the word together!

Jehoshaphat was the king of Judah at one point in time. He was known for doing what was right in the sight of the Lord. I enjoy reading the history of Jehoshaphat because: he was military-minded (a strategist), a strong leader, he learned from the mistakes of others, a visionary, preserved history, a reformer, and loyal to doing things God's way.

After reforming a nation (appointing priest, selecting judges, and creating a legal structure), the king is informed of an invasion happening in Judah and war being declared by enemies. The enemy had moved into their territory and was preparing to attack. The bible says that the king prayed to the Lord for guidance and commanded the people of Judah to fast. The people followed his instructions, dwelled in the presence of the Lord, and began to seek guidance as well. After hearing from the Lord, the king and the people began to worship and praise God. They followed the Lord's instruction. Because of their obedience to God, they received victory over the enemy and continued praising the Lord (2 Chronicles 20). Just think about this, a praise team was sent out to take the frontline during battle to sing and worship as part of God's strategy. Your praise is your weapon. This context just broke down a technique that believers can put in place during an attack. Let's magnify this divine defensive strategy once more.

Defensive Strategy
1. Prayer
2. Fasting
3. Get Into His Presence
4. Listen for Guidance from the Spirit
5. Worship The True And Living God
6. Praise
7. Obedience To God

The way communication has advance in the world today; one would tend to think that the prayer life of believers would evolve as well. Just think about how much time we spend on computers, cellphones, landlines, televisions, and radios. We send emails, text messages or instant messages, post on social networks, video chat, blog, create forums, and create web pages to get the word out. But, how much time do we spend conversing with Jesus? And, He is easier to reach, you don't have to go through any network and you want experience a drop call. King Jehoshaphat and other leaders mentioned, spent a great deal of time praying to the Lord because they realized that was the key component needed for a breakthrough. Prayer is the route to victory.

Getting into the habit of taking everything to God with prayer, supplication, and thanksgiving is one of the wisest decisions anyone can make. God knows what you are going through, He knows the sacrifices you make, and He has compassion for you. If you are obedient and follow the will of God, He will deliver you and keep you. When you have a dedicated prayer life, you have a powerful tool to break out of any stronghold. Whether your prayer is for God to grow you spiritually, heal your body, give you peace, remove fear from your heart, give you wisdom, help you to love, help you to forgive, help your ministry, help you find a job or career, renewing your mind, getting you out of an abusive situation, freeing you from captivity, giving you a heart of gratitude, transforming your life, eliminating your debt, help you stick to your budget, help you stick to your diet, self-control, mind-control, to increase your paycheck, to take authority over your finances, or to control your tongue, pray about all and everything. Don't let your faith waver. God never gives life were faith is not necessary.

When we pray about our circumstances, we experience peace. To have peace, is not saying there will be an absence of conflict. Peace is the fruit of having a relationship with Jesus. Your condition may not change immediately, but still you must continue to be a firm believer that you will win the ultimate victory with God's help.

After we have prayed, our faith must display our confidence in God. "Now faith is the substance of things hope for, yet cannot be seen" (Hebrew 11:1KJV). This means you must tell yourself, "I expect it to happen; although, these human eyes have not yet seen it take place."

Have you completed defensive strategy steps 1 through 3, and you're tired of waiting for guidance? What should you do during the waiting process? Rest. God is at His best when we're at a resting position. God does not look at resting in faith as inactivity, because it's the posture of your heart. Know that God can speak in a soft still voice or He may use someone to confirm what He has already said.

Please do not skip 'Listening'. You have to learn how to be quiet when a miracle is in progress. Do not allow your natural eyes to drain your spiritual being. Even when your progress is not evident, your faith should still be working. Never take matters into your own hands. This attitude and behavior will lead to defeat. I am speaking from experience, and I believe that I have made enough mistakes in this area for the both of us. Remain composed and trust the Holy Spirit to guide you. As human beings we have the tendency to try to help out the God who knows all, sees all, and has all power. Instead, remind yourself what He has done for you in the past and what He is continuously doing in the present.

Obedience

> "All these blessings will come on you and accompany you if you obey the Lord your God: You will be blessed in the city and blessed in the country. The fruit of your womb will be blessed, and the crops of your land and the young of your livestock-the calves of your herds and the lambs of your flocks. Your basket and your kneading trough will be blessed. You will be blessed when you come in and blessed when you come out. The Lord will grant that the enemies who rise up against you flee from you in seven. The Lord will send a blessing on your barns and on everything you put your hand to. The Lord your God will bless you in the land he is giving you." – Deuteronomy 28:2-8(NIV)

More importantly, I want you to understand that some blessings can only be obtained through obedience. When you have gained a personal relationship with the Lord, you are then able to recognize the voice of the Holy Spirit. God is not concern with your comfort, what interest Him is how well you obey. The Greek term for *obedience* is *hupakouo*. If we break this word down, *hupo* means "under" and *akouo* means "to hear", which can be translated as "submission to what is heard." Obedience is our responsibility and the outcome is God's responsibility.

Noah exemplified obedience. A man whom God found righteous was instructed to do something most individuals would consider extreme. The Word tells us that Noah did everything God commanded him. Because of his obedience, God blessed Noah and his sons (Genesis 6-10).

> "I am misunderstood because I choose to be silent; I am silent because I choose to listen; I listen because I admire He who speaks to me."

Our greatest example of obedience is Jesus Christ. He was obedient to God the Father by going to the cross. Obedience will require us to make a sacrifice. Through our obedience we demonstrate our love for God. My highest goal in life is to be faithfully obedient to God. When we are obedient, we are under authority, we are attentive, and we are carrying out a command given unto us. Keep in mind that our reward for being obedient to God will outweigh any sacrifice or adversity we endure.

On the other hand, if we choose to be disobedient, it can disqualify us from receiving our reward. Take a look at the life of Moses (Numbers 20: 6-12). Moses the man who was called to take on a difficult task, the great leader, the man who led the Exodus, the man who led the Hebrews to Mt. Sinai, the recorder of the Ten Commandments, Moses was the lawgiver, and the man that many believe towers above all others in the Old Testament, disobeyed God's command. God used Moses to bring His children out of captivity. However, during their journey to freedom even Moses disobeyed God.

The Bible tells us the children of God were complaining to the great leader because there was no water and they were physically exhausted. God commanded Moses to speak to the rock to bring forth water, but Moses chose to strike the rock twice. According to the *Life Application Study Bible* footnote, for this Moses was forbidden to enter into the Promised Land (Tyndale et al., 2005).

God looks at all of His children like He did Moses. God has a plan for us. The preferred will of God never becomes our plan without our cooperation. Every one of us has something He can use. If God sends us on an assignment, trust and believe He will be our Shepherd, our shield, and sustain us. A mission is an important cause. God desires to work through us to accomplish His will.

We must open our spiritual eyes. Satan will try to discourage us from pleasing God and fulfilling God's purpose for our lives. The enemy wants us to believe that we're not valuable to the Kingdom, that we cannot influence this world, and that we will never get out of debt or gain freedom. During our journey, Satan will try to distract us from focusing on God and obeying what He commends, but influencers know how to stay focus. Satan wants us to become content with the bondage we are in, but influencers are known for overcoming and accomplishing greatness. When we bring to remembrance the triumphs of God, we can pursue our freedom with confidence.

"I am more than what Satan thinks of me; I am more than what Satan says I am; I refuse to let Satan define who I am in any kind of way."

∿⌐∿ CHAPTER 3 ∿⌐∿
Budgeting Made Simple

E lwood Lloyd IV gives a perfect illustration on budgeting in his book *How To Finance Home Life.* The author wrote, "When an architect is consulted about the designing of a house, the first thing he wants to know is the amount which the builder can afford to spend for the house or wants to spend. He has to know his limitations in the matter of expenditure before he can go ahead with his plans. Given this figure, he then applies his knowledge and skill to design the most suitable, desirable, and substantial house which can be erected within that cost[10]..." (Lloyd, 1927, p. 28).

The *Merriam-Webster's Dictionary* defines the word *budget* as an, "Estimate of income and expenses; money available for a particular use[11]..." (1995).

How do I define a budget? A budget is like a life jacket that can keep you from drowning in debt. Some financial advisors suggest budgeting annually rather than monthly. However, if your sole purpose for budgeting is to figure out how much of your net pay (what you bring home after taxes) you're spending, to protect what you have allotted, or to increase your savings, I suggest monthly budgeting. Revisiting your budget more often can be beneficial for you.

This book will help you magnify your income and expenses, enabling you to preserve funds. Before gaining control over your finances, you must be aware of your status. "The foundation of any plan is a knowledge of the facts... upon which that plan and its execution depend. To face facts requires courage." (Lloyd, 1927, p. 29). Now, ask yourself the following questions, and answer the questions honestly. How much money do I have coming in? How much money do I have going out? How much money have I saved? How much money should I save for future emergencies or projects? If you do not know the answer to at least one of these questions, it is time to become more concerned about your finances. Your knowledge is your shield of protection. This book is your financial coach. A commitment to continuously educating yourself regarding finances can enhance your prosperity. Are you ready to take the first step?

STEP #1: Make the Decision to Create a Household Budget

The first step is making the decision to establish a budget. On my financial journey, I was encouraged to formulate a budget while going through basic training. The military provided financial training courses to help airmen better manage their income. There I learned how to properly record my income and track my expenses. After tech school, I looked at my earnings differently. I stopped throwing money away.

A Successful Budget

Detailed: The level of details depends on the expected outcome or measured performance. If you are living paycheck to paycheck, your budget worksheet should be very detailed and all encompassing.

Prior to calculating your budget, form a financial analysis. A financial analysis consists of gathering all financial data, such as current paycheck stubs, current bank statements, open loan statements, and mortgage refinance contracts. Then examine these in full detail in order to grasp a total understanding of your current finances. We may not be aware of how much debt we have created until we slow ourselves down and analyze our current situation.

Budgeting is considered a good thing because it gives you direction. Knowing your direction will give you more control over your finances. A personal budget can be used to help you live within your means, while giving you an opportunity to think of ways you can increase your income or save more. Later on down the road, you will notice how budgeting helps with money management. When you gain a full understanding of money management you will be able to spend more wisely.

No Adjustments: The only adjustments should derive from changes such as a pay raise. Too many adjustments are not good signs. Adjustments can be like trying to hit a moving target.

Revisits: Make sure you revisit your budget monthly, especially for those who live with little margins. The evaluations will leave you accountable.

Measurements: Continue to measure your assets and liabilities.

Savings: An increase in savings is a good sign. Savings can be used to pay off debt.

Step #2: Workout Your Budget Sheets

The second step is constructing your budget sheets. Now is your opportunity for financial freedom. It's time to create a fresh start. Begin this process by holding on to your receipts for six months. Use the worksheets in the back of the booklet to log your monthly take home pay, your spending, and your savings. This method will magnify your expenditures as you keep records. After this step you'll become aware of your budget and boundaries.

Recently, I was discussing a successful budget with a friend who happens to be the employee of a renowned energy company and a Certified Public Accountant in Oklahoma. As we were sharing ideas with one another, he recapped "a successful budget starts with the allocation of finances for the tithe. Give to God the first and the best and He will bless the rest." He couldn't have put it any better. Prayerfully each one of your monthly budget sheets will contain a section displaying your tithes.

Some other benefits to faithfully completing budget worksheets are forming the habit of prioritizing, organizing, paying attention to detail, and problem solving.

One day, I had received a letter from a company regarding a bill sent to a collection agency for: refusal of payment. I was confident that I had paid the bill. I gladly went to my organized

Great Financial Habits

Prioritize: Take care of priorities first. When filling in the budget worksheets, list items according to priorities. This way priorities will not be overlooked.

Organized: A budget will influence you to create a system that will ease you life.

Pay Attention To Detail: Monitor and control your spending. Address bad habits that can have an effect on your household, with the intentions of elimination.

Problem Solving: Work through details of a problem to reach a temporary or long-term solution.

budget sheets and quickly obtained the information showing the bill had been paid. I contacted the company with the date of payment, the method of payment, the check number, and the date the check had been cashed. The company's Accounts and Receivable Department updated the logbook, the credit bureaus, and apologized to me. Problem solved.

Step # 3: Stick With It

Whether you are creating a budget to gain knowledge as to where you are financially or to determine your limits, remember you have a particular goal you are trying to reach and work at it. Establishing a budget is not painful; wise people budget, large corporations budget, cities budget, states budget, and so on.

You can see evidence of a lack of budgeting by observing our own beloved country. American homeowners are still losing their homes. Tears filled my eyes as I watched the newscasts and documentaries of officials placing eviction notices on doors and escorting families out of their homes. "Borrowers, in essence allow the yokes and chains to be put on them just because they often want what they cannot afford" (Direction, 2015). Individuals signed loans that clearly did not coincide with their budgets. Stick with your budget.

Budgeting Reminders

Record: Consistently write down income and expenditures.

Examine: Revisit worksheets, spreadsheets, and receipts. Reconcile, monitor, and control income and expenditures.

Adjustments: lifestyle adjustments may be needed.

Step #4: Develop A System

Your budget worksheet objective is to show you every dollar you're spending. Having a successful budget will allow you to prepare for unexpected emergencies. At some point, we will experience a work-home conflict that can have an impact on our income, so we must be prepared. You're always preparing for a season that has not yet arrived. If you wait to prepare for this season chances are you may not live through it. Let us take heed of the words of wisdom found in the book of Proverbs relating to preparation.

> For things on earth are small, yet they are extremely wise: Ants are creatures of little strength, yet they store up their food in the summer. –Proverbs 30:24-25 (NIV)

By their habits the ants are teaching us to remain busy and productive. In the summer when the season is favorable, they are above ground gathering food and building their underground nest. Have you ever examined their system? Each group has a different task, and each task is equally important to meet their ultimate goal of survival. Some take care of the Queen ant, others dig to create new tunnels for the huge colony, another group gathers food, and other ants take care of the young. This system is structured to guarantee their survival through the winter months.

This brings me to the fourth step, which is developing a working system. This system will help you stay within your budget and achieve your goal of financial freedom.

For example, a young lady brings home $1256.67 each month. Several of her bills are due on the 1st and 15th of each month. Let's look at her monthly budget and examine her system.

Income	$1256.67
Tithes	$ 126.00
Mortgage	$ 780.00
(All) Electricity Bill	$ 125.00
	$ 40.00
Water	Differentiates
Other Expenditures	$10.00-20.00
	$1071.00
Savings	
Fixed Spending	
Disposable Income For Expenditures (Transportation, Food, Phone Service, Toiletries, and etc.)	$ 175.67

Operating account: An account with an amount sufficient to cover the bills

Personal account: An account for food and other expenditures.

The young lady's system flows like this: she has two checking accounts in which automated deposits can be made. If your system needs more discipline, you should consider having two checking accounts as well. The first account is considered the operating account, which contains funds sufficient to cover the bills. With the automatic bill paying option, the bills are withdrawn from her account monthly. Thus the young lady will stay on track and be less likely to stray from her budget.

Now, the next checking account is considered her personal account. In this account, she keeps her funds to purchase food and other expenditures. Her monthly savings is placed in her savings account.

You can choose from several different financial institutions. However, stay away from check cashing businesses that offer huge fees to cash your hard-working paychecks. A checking or savings account is a safe place to keep your money.

Step # 5: Calling Upon Mentor For Advice

Approaching your journey to freedom with a negative attitude or a lack of energy will not get you to your goal. You can make excuses or you can make progress, but you cannot do both. You must be willing to work! The closer we get to a breakthrough, the more it seems we want to hinder the process. Remember, when you feel resistance that is an indicator that you're on the right track and closer to freedom than you think. Also, this would be a perfect time to find a financial mentor. Experiencing financial bondage can be discouraging. If you are discouraged or distressed, you are going to need motivation and encouragement. Sometimes working to rebuild our financial status is overwhelming. Your mentor should be someone who wants to see you succeed in every aspect of your life. Another great tip, before you contact your mentor make a list of financial problems that you're experiencing and possible solutions and share this list with your mentor. But most of all remember, God can and will loose the shackles and set you free. Begin to speak freedom into existence.

Facts About Checking:

You can choose to do business with a bank insured with FDIC, savings and loans insured with SAIF, or a credit union insured with NCUA. These financial institutions offer different checking and savings options. Service charges vary at different rates. Select the one that fits your income. Remember, most banks insure your money up to $100,000 or up to $250,000 for regular accounts and retirement accounts.

Currently, I see fewer checkbooks and more debit cards in use. A debit card can be deemed a combination of a check and an ATM card. Both of these transactions are withdrawn from your checking account. Ask your bank if fees apply for utilizing ATMs not owned by them. With the debit card you have access to a monthly record by mail or online. However, you must keep up with receipts from your debit card. Nothing is worst than thinking you have money in your account that is not there. While some individuals may think logging expenditures is a hassle, this method tends to keep you out of the negative (red). I have plenty of funny, lighthearted stories of me going to the ATM trying to spend what has already been spent because I failed to accurately record transactions.

Banking Options

- *Direct Deposit: Your paycheck is automatically deposited to your checking account. Discuss and set up this service with your employer.*
- *Bill Pay: Services that let you pay bills at any time. Bill payments will be deducted from your checking account. This can be recurring or a one-time occurrence.*
- *E-statements, E-notices, & Check Images: Service that allows you to switch from paper to electronic account statements.*
- *Overdraft Protection: Free service designed to clear your checks with funds taken from your savings account.*

~~~ CHAPTER 4 ~~~
Gaining Control and Becoming a Good Steward

Your budget is like your compass. Your money management skills are like the equipment and tools needed for your journey. Now that you have set out a goal and have a budget in place, we can begin to focus on money management. We must work hard to make money, but we also must learn how to spend and invest our money wisely.

When I was a young girl, my grandmother occasionally asked my cousin and me to clean the homes of her senior friends. My grandmother dropped us off at each home, and we spent five hours or more cleaning. On the way out the door, we would receive between $15-20 dollars each. At that time, that seemed like a fortune to us. Soon after I arrived home, my grandmother sat us down and taught us how to tithe. *"Would a man rob God? Yet ye have robbed me. But ye say, Wherein have we robbed thee? In tithes and offerings (Malachi 3:8)."* Then she instructed us to set additional money aside for personal items. Lastly, she strongly encouraged us to save the rest of our earnings. Before I would walk away from her, she would say to me, "Don't lose it."

I am grateful I was taught the fundamentals of money management at a young age. I truly respect the parents who teach their children these life lessons as well. There was a news article that I recently read involving a mother and her child. This was a feature story that I found to be motivating and a delight to read. Each month the mother would give her child seven dollars. Then they would gather together, the mother would ask the child to give her two dollars for rent, she would ask for one dollar for utilities, a dollar for food, and another dollar for transportation. The child is only left with a few dollars; however, she is being taught a life lesson. I kept reading the article to find out that the mother would put the collected money in a savings account for her child. It is never too early to instill this form of responsibility into a child, because it may take a while for them to understand the concept. *"Train up a child in the way he should go: and when he is old, he will not depart from it (Proverbs 22:6 KJV).*

Self-Discipline

Self-discipline is a key concept to help you with money management. For the believer self-discipline is merely yielding to the Holy Spirit, and saying "no" to what our human nature wants. The Holy Spirit will not steer you wrong. Learning how to control your flesh is not easy and requires the power of the Holy Spirit.

According to Andrew Dubrin, *self-discipline* is defined as, "mobilizing ones effort and energy to stay focus on attaining an important goal (Leadership, pg.446)[16]." A wrong focus will create missed opportunities.

Need Versus Want

When making decisions, we must recognize the difference between a need and a want. A need is a necessity, something you cannot live without. A want is something you can live without, yet you desire to have.

The next time that you find yourself in a "need versus want" predicament, quickly go through the process of elimination. For example, hold up the brand new $150 purse you want, then hold up your past due electric bill, weigh the pros and cons, and then make your decision. Taking your time to make financial decisions determined by consequences is extremely important. You must have clear expectations of how your money can work for you.

Sometimes we tend to say, "I deserve those shoes, or I deserve that purse." However you must never compensate or compromise your mortgage, rent, car, or utility bills for something you can put on hold such as new shoes, a new purse, a suit, a vacation, or new furniture. Obtaining something you want should not come before your needs. Remember, small items add up quickly.

In the past, I had picked up the bad habit of smoking cigarettes. During this period there were several of times I had to make the choice between a need and a want. Such as, did I need food or did I want a cigarette. Please take a few minutes to jot down some of your *needs* and *wants*:

#	NEEDS	WANTS
e.g.	Mortgage/Rent	New Furniture
1.		
2.		
3.		
4.		

The Consumer

The smart consumer has enough discipline to take caution even during the holidays. Have you ever noticed how advertisers and marketers will subtly attempt to create a stimulus-response in consumers, especially during the holidays? A stimulus-response is when an item and an idea are place together, and an association is made between one and the other. For example, Avis has been successful in associating its name with the idea of trying harder[17] (Newsom & Haynes, 2011, p. 41).

For some consumers it will take a great measure of self-discipline to make sure that funds are available to pay the bills when those bills are due. Remember, once you begin to fall behind on paying bills, it can be difficult and stressful to catch up. Resist the urge to overspend. In other words, say no to items that will be stored away after one or two uses.

We as human beings have bad habits of making poor decisions and putting unnecessary stress upon ourselves. Stop being driven by emotions. If you really feel the need to make a purchase outside of your budget remember to pray about it and sleep on it. Usually when we delay our purchase until the following day, we come to realize that our feelings have changed towards the item.

Sadly, it's a struggle saying no, even though it can keep us debt-free. Some consumers have fallen victim to shopping addiction. They have acquired credit cards from almost all of the major retail stores. Charging purchases on numerous credit cards makes these individuals feel better, even if they cannot afford to take the credit risk. They run to the shopping center whenever they experience difficulty in life. As a result, they have accumulated such overwhelming debts that it takes them decades to recover. An obsession with shopping often becomes a massive obstacle for anyone seeking financial stability. Drowning oneself in the shopping racks due to afflictions can be unlearned. Those seeking financial freedom must rely on the Holy Spirit to stand boldly and take dominion. Say this prayer with me:

"Lord please give me the strength to bring my flesh under submission. I will no longer allow Satan to clutter my mind or stir up any emotions within me. No longer will I let the enemy keep me in bondage. Lord give me the courage to boldly say no to the flesh and yes to Your will. In Jesus Name."

The Steward

Now let us consider stewardship. Are you handling what is being placed in your care correctly? Can Christ trust you to make the right decisions regarding what He blesses you with? You should be eager to please your Savior and honored to be entrusted with whatever He gives you. The Greek word for *steward* is *oikonomos*, which means "the manager of a household or guardian[19]." Are you a good steward?

One day, I agreed to dog sit for my older sister because of her frequent trips to the hospital. My older sister had entrusted me with her dog. She had a 7 year-old, cream-colored with brown spots, male cock-a-spaniel named Droopy. As a steward, I began to love, feed, walk, play, discipline, train, and clean up after Droopy. For several days I awaked early every morning excited about taking the dog outside for a walk. One particular cold morning I dreaded getting out of bed. I was physically exhausted, frustrated, and came to resent the fact that I had agreed to take on such a demanding responsibility. I decided to open the back door and let the dog go outside alone. I made my way to the couch, sat down, and wrapped up to keep warm. When it was time to let Droopy back inside, I called his name, but there was no answer. There was no sign of my sister's precious dog. It was then that I noticed the back gate had not been secured. The dog was gone and I had failed in my task. Although heartbroken, my older sister eventually forgave me, but I had a difficult time forgiving myself.

How many believers can attest that God has left some thing of value or someone in their care, and it was not properly cared for?

There is nothing more distressing than knowing you cannot be trusted. Earning someone's trust is difficult, but rewarding. Are you dependable? It is a disappointing feeling breaking another's trust through negligence. Let's take a look at a parable that Jesus shared regarding stewardship and the building of God's Kingdom.

So he said, "There was once a man of high rank who was going to a country far away to be made king, after which he planned to come back home. Before he left, he called his ten servants and gave them each a gold coin and told them, 'See what you can earn with this while I am gone.' Now, his own people hated him, and so they sent messengers after him to say, 'We don't want this man to be our king.'" The man was made king and came back. At once he ordered his servants to appear before him, in order to find out how much they had earned. The first one came and said, 'Sir, I have earned ten gold coins with the one you gave me.' 'Well done,' he said; 'you are a good servant! Since you were faithful in small matters, I will put you in charge of ten cities.' The second servant came and said, 'Sir, I have earned five gold coins with the one you gave me.' To this one he said, 'You will be in charge of five cities.' Another servant came and said, 'Sir, here is your gold coin; I kept it hidden in a handkerchief. I was afraid of you, because you are a hard man. You take what is not yours and reap what you did not plant. He said to him, 'You bad servant! I will use your own words to condemn you! You know that I am a hard man, taking what is not mine and reaping what I have not planted. Well, then, why didn't you put my money in the bank? Then I would have received it back with interest when I returned. Then he said to those who were standing there, "Take the gold coin away from him and give it to the servant who has ten coins!" But they said to him, 'Sir, he already has ten coins!' 'I tell you,' he replied, 'that to those who have something, even more will be given; but those who have nothing, even the little that they have will be taken away from them. Luke 19:12-26 GNT.

Every believer is given gifts for which we are responsible. Whether the gifts appear to be large or small from a human perspective, the way we decide to use the gifts is solely up to us. We must have enough faith, courage, and strength to utilize the gifts for the building of the Kingdom. This is your year to be bold enough to act!

Don't be like the servant who was critical and chose not to invest the gift and therefore was penalized. The servant was given a free gift and yet decided not to utilize it.

Are you guilty of saying, "I can't do this as well as him or her," so you choose not to use your gift? How often do you let God down because you do not value what is important to Him or mismanage what He has given you? Can God

Money-Saving Tips

- Using coupons can help you save money to add to your savings account.

- Taking your lunch to work instead of eating out can help you save, add to your savings account, and improve your diet.

- Carpooling can be beneficial for you and your coworkers.

- Buying groceries in bulk allows you to proportion your food, based on needs.

- Reducing unused phone or cable features helps you add money to your savings account.

rely on you? If we are found faithful over a few things, God will make us ruler over many (Matthew 25:21 KJV). Here is something you must know about

- Catching a matinee rather than an evening movie can save you money.

God: He won't let you skip courses; there are some paths you must take. Don't strive to have the best, strive to be the best and do the best with what God has given.

> Much is required from the person to whom much is given; much more is required from the person to whom much more is given. –Luke 12:48b GNT

CHAPTER 5
Saving for a Cause

During my college internship at the Oklahoma Society of Certified Public Accountants, I learned how to make my savings account's money grow. "To have money saved is interesting, whether the amount saved be large or small. But the saving, the current, concrete act of saving of itself is uninteresting and somewhat of a bore to most of us unless we have some definite reason for saving.[21]" (Lloyd, p. 224).

Savings has its importance for several reasons. In this book we have already discussed two reasons: help prepare us for unexpected expenses and to attain a goal. In this chapter you will learn various techniques and financial routes to take to help increase your savings.

The Art of Saving

When I purchased my car during college, it was the best car I had ever owned. Nearly ten years later, friends and family teased me, and tried to persuade me to purchase

Savings 101

1. Make sure you choose a good bank or credit union for your savings. Saving at home is a bad idea.

41

an up-to-date vehicle. I guess they wanted me to keep up with the latest trend. However, they failed to understand that I didn't want the burden of a car payment. My car was finally paid off, and I had been enjoying the financial freedom of no car payments. When there is nothing wrong with what you possess, why go into debt? Instead, I learned to put the amount I would spend on a monthly car payment into a savings account. Focusing on savings and paying off your debts could put you in the brackets of early retirement. We can benefit from using a portion of our savings to decrease our debts.

Savings v.s. Checking

Investing your money in different savings options is a terrific notion. Unlike your checking account

2. There are different types of savings, and you're allowed to have more than one savings account. The question is what type of savings will benefit both you and your family.

3. Allow your money to accumulate more wealth from interest. Always inquire about the financial institution's interest rates. Interest can be defined as money that the bank pays out to you for saving and allowing your money to be loaned to others.

4. Self-discipline will help you refrain from dipping into your savings until you reach your goal.

that decreases with withdrawals, your savings account will increase with deposits. Remember, even loose change adds up. How much money are you currently saving from your income? Are you living off of 80% and saving 20%? Are you living off 80%, tithing 10%, and saving 10%?

Have a plan for your savings. Whether your goal is paying off credit cards, saving for college tuitions or retirement, paying off medical bills, or fixing up your home, savings must be at the core of your financial plan.

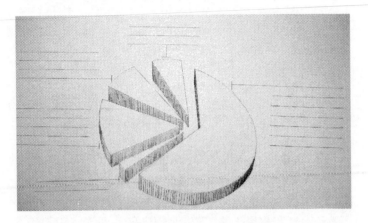

A FEW SAVING JARGON & SAVING OPTIONS:

- *Disposable Money~* Is the money you have left after you have paid all of your bills. It is very important to have either a short-term or a long-term savings goal for this money.
- *Standard Savings Account~* Offered with a low monthly, minimum balance required and is FDIC insured. These funds can be taken out at anytime to assist with emergencies and/or goals.
- *Certificates of Deposit (CDs)~* This is a special type of deposit with low-risk. Your insured money will be placed aside for a length of time and will bear a maturity date. The interest depends on the length of the term. If you withdraw currency before the term ends, you will be penalized. These funds can assist with short-term and/or long-term goals. A suggestion is to use a portion of your income tax return, to purchase a CD.

- *U.S. Savings Bonds~* The Federal Government supports these bonds. In return for your purchase the government agrees to pay you back with interest on the future redemption date. I love to purchase these for birthdays or holidays. In the long run, your child will benefit more from a bond than a new toy. Instead of buying several toys, try purchasing one or two along with a savings bond.
- *401(k)/403(b)~* These are pretax contributions that reduce your current taxable income. Funds can be invested in a variety of ways. The funds are not taxed until they are withdrawn. Ask your company about these retirement savings. In addition, these savings can also be used before retirement if you experience financial hardship.
- *Traditional or Roth IRA's~* These are personal savings plans and great ways to save for retirement. The difference between these two IRA's is the time you pay your taxes. Do you wish to pay taxes now or later?

With the Traditional IRA, you can save on taxes now. This type of savings plan gives you a tax break when you make contributions, and then when you get ready to withdraw you are taxed.

With the Roth IRA, it is just the opposite. You don't get a tax break when you make contributions., but when you get ready to withdraw no taxes are paid.

Educational IRA ~ These savings option must be opened in the child's name. This IRA must be used for educational purposes only. Such as tuition, housing, books and etc.

CHAPTER 6

Preparing for a New Path

You just received confirmation from the Holy Spirit on taking a new path. Although financial planning can be daunting, you are excited about the challenge. Is the Holy Spirit leading you to unite with the love of your life, to start your own business, or begin on the path back to school? Jesus holds the truth about your future. The plans and blessings that Christ have for your life are for you, and no one can stop Him from making these happen on your behalf. You just have to take the first step of obedience. The higher you climb the better view you will have.

God-Given-Instructions

> And Saul, yet breathing out threatenings and slaughter against the disciples of the Lord, went unto the high priest, And desired of him letters to Damascus to the synagogues, that if he found any of this way, whether they were men or women, he might bring them bound unto Jerusalem. And as he journeyed, he came near Damascus: and

suddenly there shined round about him a light from heaven: And he fell to the earth, and heard a voice saying unto him, Saul, Saul, why persecutest thou me? And he said, Who art thou, Lord? And the Lord said, I am Jesus whom thou persecutest: it is hard for thee to kick against the pricks. And he trembling and astonished said, Lord, what wilt thou have me to do? And the Lord said unto him, Arise, and go into the city, and it shall be told thee what thou must do -Acts 9:1-6 KJV

Saul, a very educated Pharisee with strong Jewish beliefs, once lived a life persecuting Christians. During his journey to help put a stop to Christianity, he met Jesus and was given a new path to take. Christ had other plans for Saul. Saul, the prevailing persecutor, became Paul, the powerful preacher. Jesus directed Saul to change his career and then changed his reputation.

Paul became empowered by the Lord, allowed the Holy Spirit to use him, performed miracles, spoke truth with boldness, presented the Gospel to the Gentiles, discipled believers, and wrote more than half of the New Testament. When we are given instructions from the Lord it is in our best interest to follow them. Following such instruction will require strength and courage. Most people are incredible starters, but not good at finishing. Any great vision that comes from God will always be opposed. There are four fierce oppositions that you may come across on your new path. Those are accusation, discouragement, fear, and frustration. This is when courage and strength will be needed the most.

A Career Change

Some people resist change because it can be too overwhelming, difficult, complicated, or time consuming. Change and comfort can never coexist. When the "Great I Am" dwells within you, then your diction should become "I Can".

I have a friend who received confirmation from the Holy Spirit to pursue the path of becoming an entrepreneur. She created a business plan for the transition, prepared, and established a business doing

<u>Financial Advice</u>

Concurrently build time into your schedule for financial planning. Your spouse is not a financial plan.

exactly what she loves. Before she resigned from her job, she built up her clientele and made sure she had supporting income. Her husband was extremely encouraging. Because she planned and prepared for the new path, she eliminated the burden of her husband handling all of the bills himself. She allowed the Spirit of the Lord to guide her and crown her head with knowledge and wisdom to properly plan for the transition. Her career changed, but her trust in God didn't.

Ordered Steps

> The steps of a good man are ordered by the Lord: and he delighteth in his way. – Psalms 37:23 (KJV)

Everyday, I ask the Lord to order my steps and allow His will to be done. I want to be found guilty in finding delight in following Christ. Often we do not have the luxury of fully preparing for the path God leads us down. Often we sit down, contemplate, make plans and have everything mapped out. Then the Lord rearranges our entire agenda.

Being in God's purpose does not necessarily mean that you will not experience difficulties. Remember you may go through some storms, but you're not staying in the storm. Maybe your new path appears to be gloomy. Were you forced into retirement? Did you wake up headed to work only to receive a pink slip shortly after arriving? Did your spouse come home one day to announce he wanted a divorce? Have the negative emotions of resentment, unforgiveness, and offense taken root in your life? Uproot these immediately, and cast them away. God can take a night season (a moment despair), and birth hope in your life.

"Some circumstances are beyond our control. If we fail to see the hand of God behind our circumstances, we will be vulnerable to confusion, frustration, bitterness, anger, and despair.[23]" (DeMoss, p.101).

The Lord knows where He is leading you. When His Spirit speaks to us and leads us to unfamiliar places, it can be overwhelming. But, every place the Lord sends us becomes extraordinary with Him.

> To have faith is to be sure of the things we hope for, to be certain of the things we cannot see. – Hebrews 11:1 GNT

The word "faith" in Greek is pistis[24]. Faith is one of the fruit of the Spirit. We must learn to rest in faith. This rest is our willingness to trust God. The Lord wants us to trust in Him. He is unwavering, trustworthy, and loyal. When we rest in God, we'll find the rest of God. Be filled with joy as His Spirit directs your footsteps! His plan for our lives is far better than our own. We must listen as His Spirit speaks.

Remember, the Lord does things differently than we do. Therefore just like my friend and others, we must trust Him completely. After all He does have the master plan! As the Lord prepares and takes you down a new path, make sure you put total trust in Him. My friends do not falter as you travel in a new direction. You were created to prosper, and to be the head and not the tail (Deuteronomy 28:44).

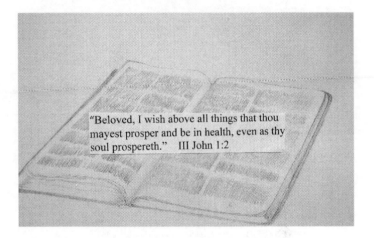

"Beloved, I wish above all things that thou mayest prosper and be in health, even as thy soul prospereth."   III John 1:2

<u>When Starting or Buying a Business:</u>

- Do your research and figure out who's the competition.
- Create a SWOT analysis (Strengths, Weaknesses, Opportunities, Threats).
- Create short-term and long-term goals.
- Create a great business plan (introduction, description, goals, and marketing).
- Intellectual Property such as Copyrights, Patents, Trademarks, and Trade Secrets acts as a business asset
- If buying an existing business, search out the reasons the previous owner sold.

- When you buy a franchise, you buy marketing support and other assistance.
- Think of a name for your business (check with the **Secretary of State** to make sure the name doesn't already exist).
- Choose an entity for your business (sole proprietor, partnership, LLP, LLC, etc…).
- Register your business name
- File **Articles of Incorporation**
- Obtain tax identification numbers and permits
- File taxes
- Consider using social media (Facebook, Twitter, Instagram, Snapchat, Linkedin, YouTube, and Pinterest to build company presence
- Research and learn more about types of funding (Equity, Lending, Reward-Based, Donations and ICO)

When Changing Jobs:

- Discover how often the company gives evaluations, performance reviews, and pays increases.
- Learn if and/or how often overtime is given.
- Ask about commissions, bonuses, and profitable sharing plans.
- Don't forget to rollover your 401(k).

When Going to College

- See if you qualify for financial aid.
- Inquire about the work-study program.
- Apply for scholarships (due to the lack of applicants many programs stop funds).

- See if your job has an educational program in place that will help fund college.
- Think about taking foreign language courses as an elective (being bilingual can earn you more money annually on a job).

When Buying A Car

- First ask yourself if you really need a new vehicle.
- If you do, choose a car that fits your needs (consider also the fuel economy), and budget.
- Determine the right price (find out the invoice price).
- Shop around for the best deal.
- Ask about special finance programs.
- Beware of overpriced additions.

When Merging Money Due to Marriage

- Discuss your financial goals with each other (it is important to discuss how you two will handle your finances; communication is vital before and during marriage).
- Be open: know each other's financial history and credit score
- Make a list of short-term and long-term goals (determine the importance of these goals).
- Create a budget.
- Decide whether you will have joint or separate bank accounts (if joint accounts: discuss which financial institution(s) would be best) .
- Decide whether to keep insurance separate or join together with better coverage.

When Planning for Retirement

- Seek the help of a trustworthy-credible financial advisor to understand your retirement plan.

Different Types of Business Roles

- Creativity Specialist
- Public Relations
- Marketing & Sales
- Book Keeping
- Traffic Manager

Marketing Secrets

- Consistency
- Commitment
- Creativity
- Measurements
- Repetition

Business Problem-Solving

- Identify the Issue
- Get to the Root of the Issue
- Find & Implement a Solution

CHAPTER 7

Getting Out of Debt

C hrist paid the ultimate price for us at the cross. His innocence claimed our guilt. We were in debt to sin, and our sentence was death; however, Christ gave His life in our place. He redeemed us, and now we have the gift of eternal life. Sometimes we seem to forget about the demeaning acts committed toward our Savior. The people shouted loudly, out of hate, "Crucify Him" (Matthew 27:23). They insulted and mocked Him (Matthew 27:29). These same individuals had witnessed and heard about His supernatural miracles. Our Savior was whipped and beaten (Mark 14:65). Physically tired and weak, Christ was nailed to a cross. His body stretched and ached from all the pain. His blood came streaming down.

> Jesus answered, "I am the way and the truth and the life. No one comes to the Father except through me.
> John 14:6 NIV

He died for our salvation. Knowing this brings me to a shout. Hallelujah! I am so thankful for what Christ has done for us on Calvary. How does it make you feel to know that you had a death sentence, but Christ paid your debt in full? Some people do not fully realize that we are no longer dead to sin; we have been brought with a price. I can recall reading a story about a farmer whose sheep was tied up and stolen. A police officer found the sheep lying in a ditch, covered with dirt on the side of the road. The officer called the farmer to the scene and informed the farmer that the sheep was dead. The farmer went down into the ditch and realizes the sheep was still alive. The farmer untied the sheep and commanded the sheep to get up. But the sheep just laid in the ditch as if it was still bound. Then the farmer pulled the sheep's legs apart and stood the sheep up and gave another command. The sheep finally moved out of the ditch. We must stop living out of our fallen identity and begin living out of our redeemed identity. If the enemy can distort our identity, then he can keep us immobilized. Brothers and sisters we are no longer bound by sin and it is time we realize that truth and move out of the pit.

When Jesus was in Capernaum (a place where He spent a great deal of time teaching and performing miracles), He had an encounter with a man that had also lost his identity and was bound (Luke 5:17-26 KJV). The man was a paralytic brought to Jesus by four great friends. I considered the paralyzed man's friends to be great because they had enough brotherly love for the man that it initiated their faith. They were determined to see their friend healed. How many friends are you surrounded by that no longer wants to see you as the victim, but wishes to see you victorious? When the bound man was placed in front of Jesus, the first thing Jesus did was give the man an identity. Some translations of the bible have Jesus calling him: man, son, or friend. Nevertheless, the palsy man was giving a new identity by Christ. This world will try to label you everything except what the Lord has called you. Every time the world wants to dominate someone it puts a label on the individual or group of people. But, Christ has calls us is sons and daughters.

Jesus didn't just come to earth to die; He came to be our Savior. No one is worthy to come to the Father, but through

His Son (John 14:6). As we accept Christ, God accepts us. Jesus didn't give His life, so that we can be informed, but transformed. While the gospel didn't cost us anything, it will definitely demand everything. Our Lord is jealous; we cannot commit ourselves to Him and slide back into the world. The lifestyle of Jesus is meant to be duplicated. It is in a Christian's nature to be like Christ. He doesn't just do amazing things, but He invites us to be apart of the amazement.

Hit with Financial Debt

I woke up headed to work one morning, joyous and expecting a miracle. That day I decided to fast. Doing good on time, I figured I had enough time to stop by the Post Office first. The morning stop would have freed me up that evening. While I was driving snowflakes began to fall. Each one dissolved as it hit the car window. I thought *Wow, God was so amazing.* Suddenly, the Volkswagen in front of me spun out of control, clipping my frontend and sending me head first into the wall of the highway. It didn't stop there, I vaguely remember colliding with another car behind me. I was transported to the hospital. Sometimes we find ourselves being hit with debt. The driver of the vehicle was uninsured. The hospital bills tallied up to more than $40,000. "Uninsured Motorist" (auto insurance coverage) is a small investment that you will come to thank yourself for later. My insurance agent informed me that more than 30% of American drivers are uninsured. How troubling.

I never made it to the Post Office, I never made it to work, but I did receive my miracle. My life was spared! This was a sure indicator that God still have some work for me to accomplish. I just stop my to tell you that your miracle maybe found in the middle of your mess.

Understanding Debt

Let me honest, some times in order to be consider an expert on subject matters we must first experience a few things. Often when God gets ready to add substance and depth to our lives, He places us in pressure points. There will be times when you will win and other times you will learn. When I begin writing this book all kind of chaos begin to break lose in my life. I begin having intense welfare, it was a sign that I was on the right track and the enemy had discerned my future. The enemy will always try to use problems to block you from your promise. As long as there are broken people in the world we should be sharing the gospel and our life-changing stories. People are hungry for Christ. We must be willing to give ourselves. Weariness can replace our willingness. Your calling has to become more valuable to you than anything else in this world. There is a generation rising up that does not know Christ. We are placing our children in the hands of ungodly institutions. We must fight for our children! Especially when they cannot fight for themselves.

Since, you have built financial tenacity into your life (seeking ways to resolve your debt), it is time to pay off your financial debts slowly.

Financial debt occurs when a borrower receives money from a lender. There are two forms of financial debt, secured and unsecured.

Secured debt is back by collateral (an asset or lien guarantees this debt). An example of secured debt would be your mortgage and/or car loan.

On the other hand, unsecured debt is not secured by an asset or lien. Examples of this type of debt would be credit cards, medical bills, and utility bills.

The majority of individual unsecured debt comes from credit cards and loans. I noticed institutions are quickly targeting students before they graduate from high school seeking to lure them into debt. We must educate students on financial literary. Equipping them with wisdom and knowledge will prepare them for the future. Without the right information, your inspiration will die. Here are a few tips to learn as you move forward:

Moving Forward:
Always be clear about what you're pursuing (the only thing worst than being blind is having sight, but little to no vision)
Always be clear about why you're pursuing (know the why behind your mission)
Always be clear about when you're to pursue it
Always be clear as to who you should take along with you as you're pursuing (this may require you to cut off individuals that drag you back into old experiences or from individuals with unbelief)

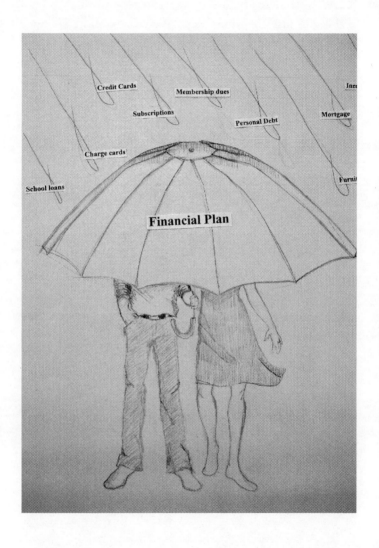

Nicole Ford and Erica Russell

The rich ruleth over the poor, And the borrower is servant to the lender. -Proverbs 22:7 (KJV)

Facing the Facts

Do you remember the woman at the well? She too had to face some important facts. This woman started her day just like we do sometimes. She was going through the motions not expecting a miracle to occur. There was a void in her life as well that she spent her time and her energy trying to hide. The bible tells us Jesus was passing through Samaria and He takes a moment to rest at a well (John 4:4-42 KJV). Christ meets a woman that has come to the same place to draw water. Please take note that every time God wants to increase our life He brings someone into our lives. Jesus asked the woman for a drink and the she stated a fact. She mentioned that Christ was a Jew and she was a Samaritan. This was indeed factual and Jesus himself knew it to be true. However, Jesus also knew more important facts about the woman. Like the fact the woman had emptiness inside, or the fact she was living in denial. It wasn't until the lady took off her mask and was truthful with Jesus; then after, she was delivered. The Lord cannot bless the fake you.

I could go through life as if it was my grand stage. With dissimulation I mosey to work, strutted in church and marched through the halls of my own homes, but I was torn-up inside. I wanted to pretend everything was all right, hoping that my debt and financial hardship would somehow disappear. I expected the Mary Kay, Clinique, and COVERGIRL products to hide my financial woes. However, the truth is that I was broken and had several restless nights. I was filled with worry and anxiety. I made my requests known unto the Lord, begging Him to take me out of my messes, instead of asking Him for the strength to get through the difficult times. I remember the day I decided to fight debt head on. Arriving home after work, I opened my mail and looked at my loans. I hadn't realized how large my debt had become. In fact, it was so bad that I had began to cry. I was so discouraged. It seemed as if I would never have enough resources to resolve my debt. I didn't like owing people at all. At that very moment I was fed up with my mountainous debt.

I had reached for a small booklet regarding eliminating debt. Brand new. The pages had never been turned. It had been given to me by a former teacher years before. Upon receiving the booklet, never did it cross my mind that I would need to read the information inside and apply it to my own life. As I turned the pages, wisdom leaped out. I was given insight to speak to my debt and command it to leave. I grabbed all my credit card debt, past due utility billing statements, and student loan papers. I laid my hands on top of the pile, and I remember saying this prayer:

> "Lord, I have no clue as to what I am doing. I have made a complete mess; however, I know that you can hover over my mess and straighten it all out. I invite you in this area of my life. Give me the wisdom and knowledge to deal with my finances accordingly. In the name of Jesus, I call these debts paid in full! Debt, you are gone and no longer exist!"

At that very moment I believed every word that came out of my mouth. Then I decided to act in faith. I refused to be defeated. No longer could the enemy keep me in a stronghold. I demanded to be freed. You cannot count yourself out! The bible clearly states that if we lift up Christ, then He will begin to draw. If you place the Lord and the position He belongs, then He will draw you out of bondage, poverty, addiction, oppression, depression or whatever horrifying condition you may be in. The best is not in your past; it is in your today. In order for you to enter into your promised land, you must put your faith into action.

Reprogramming Your Mind

The Israelites were delivered from captivity in Egypt in one night; nevertheless, it took the nation 40 years to get the ways of Egypt out of their mind frame. Sometimes we can be physically free, but still mentally enslaved. It's good to remember the lessons of the past (if you don't remember, you will repeat), but don't let the past stunt the growth of your future. Although the nation was free, they wondered in the wilderness for four decades because they refused to change their mind set. Brothers and sisters that is a hard pill to swallow, knowing that God can bring us out of one mess, but old habits can put us right back in another mess. We must ask the Holy Spirit to renew our minds and change our thinking pattern even if our circumstances don't seem to change.

When God raises you up and out, it doesn't mean that you want deal with other problems. The Lord doesn't just want to deliver you from something; He wants to transform you into something great. It is not His will to have you going through a never-ending cycle of craziness. But, it is His will to make you an overcomer. There were five things that posed as a challenge for the Israelites then and for us now: trouble, persecution, worry & anxiety, deceit, and lust.

> Since you have accepted Christ Jesus as Lord, live in union with him. Keep your roots deep in him, build your lives on him, and become stronger in your faith, as you were taught. And be filled with thanksgiving. See to it, then, that no one enslaves you by means of the worthless deceit of human wisdom, which comes from the teachings handed down by human beings and from the ruling spirits of the universe, and not from Christ. – Colossians 2:6-8(GNT)

You have been delivered from bondage to worship. Before you accepted Christ, you were your own captain, you chose your own path, you made your own choices, and you were the chooser of your own destiny. But now that you have accepted Jesus, you have given Him complete authority. Your next bold move will call for His supernatural power. The process of becoming will: take place in a hostile environment, involve how to navigate through troubles, will teach us God's way, and will reveal His goodness.

Eliminating debt or experiencing freedom may seem like a slow and tedious process. But, hopefully you come to fully understand the importance of reprogramming your thinking. You may have to resort to cut backs in order to gain financial freedom.

You must delete the secular images the world has stored in your mind. We are told by society that our lives should focus on materialism. So then while pursuing the dream others have set out for us, we often accumulate debt. We have all fallen victim to this deception. A worldview is a set of assumptions, beliefs, and values, which produces individual action or reaction to human culture. A Christian worldview is when you not only believe and value the history regarding the creation, the fall and the redemption, but you believe it sets in place the way things should be. What is God calling you to do or become?

Resolving Your Debt

If your debts need immediate attention, seek a financial advisor. Make an appointment for a face-to-face meeting. Always seek wise counsel before you make financial assumptions. Some financial advisors working at banking institutions are even willing to consult with you for free. Speak with them and see if you can benefit from debt consolidation. Plan a strategy to eliminate your debt, and then be determine to follow through.

I focused on diminishing my debt. I slowly paid each bill one by one. Always pay off your small debts first, and get a credit report annually. Some older debts may no longer show on your credit report. If I could not pay on a bill right away, I called the company and was honest with them about my financial status. I made payment arrangements with the companies. I wrote out 'Promise to Pay' statements and sent it to the companies. A year later a portion of my debt was gone. Three years later another portion was gone. Within five years God had delivered me and given me financial freedom. Triumphantly, I was debt free!

I strongly advise you not to let your debt discourage you. Learn from your mistakes. You will overcome and become debt-free if you persist.

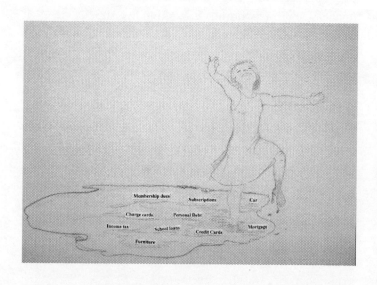

Nicole Ford and Erica Russell

CHAPTER 8

Worship & Giving

> "But the time is coming and is already here, when by the power of God's Spirit people will worship the Father as he really is, offering him the true worship that he wants. God is Spirit, and only by the power of his Spirit can people worship him as he really is." John 4:23-24 GNT

The Greek word for *"worship"* is *sebasma*[25] (Renner, 2003). It is a verb meaning "reverence, veneration, worship, or adore". As believers we are commanded to worship God and Him only (Luke 4:8). We must seek God with a purpose to worship. When we worship God, we give Him our undivided attention and focus on who God is. It is imperative to refrain from worshipping what God has created or blessed us with (Romans 1:25). So the question is not if people worship, but who or what are people worshiping? Are you worshiping your business, ministry, cars, sex and other things of that nature? Don't exchange worshiping the Creator, for worshiping His creation. There are some people who worship a god that they have to pick up and carry around. But, the true and living God doesn't need to be lifted up as a matter of fact He has to carry us. Please note, an idol will never surprise you. Worship can be viewed as a lifestyle and something you present. Let's take a moment to examine two different occasions were worship takes place and then discuss the acts.

> Then came to him the mother of Zebedee's children with her sons, worshipping him, and desiring a certain thing of him. (Matthew 20:20 KJV)

Now let's read the next example:

> There came unto him a woman having an alabaster box of very precious ointment, and poured it on his head, as he sat at meat. (Matthew 26:7 KJV)

Both ladies worshipped the Lord. But one-woman only worship Christ because she expected something in return. The passage recorded the mother of James and John (two of Christ's disciples), being motivated to worship Christ due to the fact that she was seeking high positions for her sons. Was her motive wrong? Which one of these examples displays the form of worship that you often give to Christ?

We can learn the act of true worship from the stories of Mary (Lazarus's sister) in the New Testament. In fact, Jesus tells us that the way Mary worshipped will be spoken about wherever the Gospel is preached (Matt. 26:13). True worship is always the result to recognizing who God really is. Mary's act of worship involved unselfishness. True worship is an unselfish act. Jesus was frequently in the presence of Mary and Martha and, Mary was frequently positioned at the feet of Jesus.

True worship requires a personal relationship with Him. You cannot sincerely worship whom you don't know (John 4:22a). Mary knew Jesus because she spent time with Him.

Mary took expensive pure ointment and began to pour it on Jesus the Christ. The same ointment was used to anoint Kings[26]. Mary understood the purpose that Jesus had to fulfill on this earth. Christ accepted and honored her sacrificial gift of worship.

Mary's worship consisted of:

* Love
*Adoration
* Purity
*Unselfishness
*Humblenss
^Devotion
*Respect
*Sacrifice

During our sacred worship we must empty ourselves before Christ by giving our entire beings unto Him. The perfume was costly like her priceless worship. The smell of the perfume filled the entire house (John 12:3) in the same way worship illuminates our entire temple. When you worship you pour out your devotion onto Him.

At that moment, Jesus looked at more than just her act; He also accepted the love and devotion given to Him. Mary was prepared and determined to worship her King. Authentic worship humbles the heart. This story is a great reminder that true worship knows how to extend the love of God. To learn more about worship read John 4, as Jesus teaches us about what worship is like. My friends always remember that worship reconnects you to Christ.

Worshipping Christ After Difficulties

You were delivered from whatever dreadful state you were in, so that you could worship. Worshipping Jesus before and after experiencing difficulties can help restore your joy. Do not let any thing or anyone interfere with your worship (Matt. 21:12).

Worship can take place at your church, at your home, at your job, or even in your car. There is not a set place. We can never live life to its fullest without being in the presence of the Lord. Often times we are searching for principles, encouragement, or how-tos, when we need to be experiencing the presence of the Lord. When you get into the presence of the Lord, you may come to find out that the Jesus you think you know is keeping you from the Jesus you need to know.

The Gift of Giving

> Not that I desire your gift; what I desire is that more be credited to your account. – Philippians 4:17 (NIV)

The term blessing is deemed two-fold; two transactions are present, which is giving and receiving. The bible tells us repeatedly the importance of giving. God gave His Son; His son gave His life; Now what are you willing to give Him? Your breakthrough will be wrapped up in your giving. Your heart will always regulate your hands. For example if you have a heart for animals, you may invest time and money into fostering pets or being an advocate for finding pets a loving home. If you're proeducation, you may study to become a teacher. Changing the lives of students inside the classroom. When your heart gets full, it moves you to take certain actions. The love and passion in your heart will help sustain what you're holding in your hands. Remember you can give without love, but never can you love without giving.

So many people don't know Jesus and need the help of Christians. Share Christ with others! Give up some of your time to allow your testimony to help deliver someone from his or her bondage. Try not to be insensitive to the needs of others. Be willing to fulfill all of God's directions (Matt. 23:23).

When I first began to teach Women's Bible Study at my church, my Uncle told me, "Our goal is to make bad men better, better men productive, and keep productive men encouraged." As Christians we must be concerned about the souls of people (Proverbs 11:30). So many people our lost and others are lukewarm (Revelation 3:16). If you know someone who has lost his or her passion for Christ, help him or her recover it. When individuals become slothful, they begin to lose momentum. A lack of momentum can make small hills look like mountains. Please try to help the individual identify why and when did he or she begin to become slothful or lose momentum. Also, try to help the individual properly discern the season he or she is in (some people look for harvest when they are in the sowing season). Momentum comes back with remembering the goodness of the Lord.

Is Satan trying to stop you from giving to your church or other ministries? Has your heart been hardened toward generously giving to help spread the Good News? God uses His children to plant financial gifts into churches, prison ministries, food ministries, and other various ministries to help advance the building of the Kingdom of God. If God has blessed you financially, don't just sit on your financial blessings but be a blessing to others and the church. Do not worry about the size of your financial seed. Giving a generous offering to the church ensures the Good News spreads inside the church, throughout the community, and surrounding areas. When you give to those in need, you benefit as well. If you are considering planting a financial seed in a ministry that you are not familiar with, do some research to find out what the ministry is accomplishing or planning to accomplish.

When this book was being written, there were several

publishing companies making us offers. With that being said, there was a publishing company that identified themselves with being Christian based. We grew excited about partnering with a local company. After meeting other authors that had work with the company; eventually, we agreed to work with this company. We put in years of writing, compiling creative marketing strategies, and working with one of the best illustrators in our area. Soon after our project had gone into stores, the company was under investigation. Executive leaders were charge by the Attorney General for several crimes. It took me a while to gain lost momentum. If your dreams don't get you up, your dreams will not move others. I had to encourage myself to continue with the vision the Lord had given me. Brothers and sisters we live in a world were sadly people are not perfect, please make sure you ask for guidance concerning the company you're partnering with or giving to. It broke my heart to witness criminals try to capitalize on Christ and mislead believers; but we must forgive. If we are humble enough to ask God for forgiveness, we must be spiritual enough to forgive others. Never give up on yourself or dreams even if you experience setbacks. You must give your time; use your spiritual gifts and talents to help expand God's Kingdom.

Gaining
Wealth

God's

Way

You may say to yourself, "My power and the strength of my hands have produced this wealth for me." But remember the Lord your God, for it is he who gives you the ability to produce wealth, and so confirms his covenant, which he swore to your ancestors, as it is today. - Deuteronomy 8:17-18(NIV)

END NOTES

God promised to set us free from bondage. We must have faith in God's Word, be obedient, use the wisdom we have garnered for our freedom, and take corrective measurements to remain free. Everyday that you are fortunate to wake up make sure you: own your day, arrange your day with the Spirit of the Lord, and occupy your day.

Many people can explain theology, but fail to have a true connection with Christ. This is far from a get rich quick book; instead, this booklet encourages the reader to get right with God, place Him first, straighten out priorities, and become better managers. When we do, then true wealth building will come spiritually and financially. I desire for you to be prosperous. I want you to be rich toward God by eliminating bad habits, and turning from whatever distracts you from Him. Never forget that your true wealth is in God. My friends quit looking for an unexplainable God to do explainable things and get ready for something supernatural to transpire.

Scriptures on Finances

"Will a mere mortal rob God? Yet you rob me. "But you ask, 'How are we robbing you?' "In tithes and offerings. You are under a curse—your whole nation—because you are robbing me. Bring the whole tithe into the storehouse, that there may be food in my house. Test me in this," says the Lord Almighty, "and see if I will not throw open the floodgates of heaven and pour out so much blessing that there will not be room enough to store it. -Malachi 3:8-10 (NIV)

So if you have not been trustworthy in handling worldly wealth, who will trust you with true riches? – Luke 16:11 (NIV)

The Lord will grant you abundant prosperity-in the fruit of your womb, the young of your livestock and the crops of your ground-in the land he swore to your ancestors to give you. The Lord will open the heavens, the storehouse of his bounty, to send rain on your land in season and to bless all the work of your hands. You will lend to many nations but will borrow from none. The Lord will make you the head, not the tail. If you pay attention to the commands of the Lord your God that I give you this day and carefully follow them, you will always be at the top, never at the bottom. – Deuteronomy 28:11-13 (NIV)

Supporting Scripture

For it is with your heart that you believe and are justified, and it is with your mouth that you profess your faith and are saved. – Romans 10:10 (NIV)

But since you excel in everything —in faith, in speech, in knowledge, in complete earnestness and in the love we have kindled in you—see that you also excel in this grace of giving. – 2 Corinthians 8:7 (NIV)

His faith did not leave him, and he did not doubt God's promise; his faith filled him with power, and he gave praise to God. – Romans 4:20 (GNT)

Prayers

Lord, I would like to thank you for saving me. I realize that breaking strongholds will not be easy, so I am asking you to strengthen me. Order my steps dear Lord. Teach me to be obedient and walk in love. In the mighty name of Jesus I pray.

Lord, please help me control myself whenever I get tempted to do something not pleasing in your sight or purchase something that will cause a financial setback in my life. For your word says that if I have faith as small as a mustard seed I can speak to a mulberry tree and command it to move. Help me to stay focus and achieve your plans for my life. In the mighty name of Jesus I pray.

Lord, I surrender to your Spirit. Your Word says whatsoever I bind on earth is bound and heaven, and whatsoever I loose on earth is loosed in heaven. I bind every obstacle set out to keep me from spiritual and financial prosperity. In the mighty name of Jesus I pray.

Confessions

Lord, I confess that I am weak, yet you are strong. Therefore help me to change my outlook on life and see things through spiritual eyes. There is no place for negativity to reside within me, remove it and fill me with Your love. I have prayed for financial freedom and prosperity, I believe that I will receive. In the mighty name of Jesus it's done.

As God's Spirit leads me to make wise and prosperous decisions regarding my finances, I realize that as I give it is given unto me, good measure, pressed down, shaken together and running over. In the mighty name of Jesus it's done.

ABOUT THE AUTHOR

Nicole Ford was reared in Oklahoma by her grandmother, a true guardian. During her senior year in high school, Nicole studied nursing. After graduating, she decided to continue nursing school, later obtaining her license as a Registered Medical Assistant. Nicole worked several years in the medical field. Thereafter, she joined the United States Armed Forces. During enlistment, she decided to return to college. Nicole earned a Bachelor of Arts Degree in Journalism with a Minor in Public Relations. Before Nicole separated from the military as a Sergeant, she earned several prestigious awards such as 'Airman of the Year,' and trained numerous airmen.

Nicole Ford is a passionate bible teacher. She is a teacher for the State of Oklahoma, the founder of Nicole Ford & Co., a public relations firm, and the founder of Carrie Octavia Ford Scholarship Foundation. She remains active in community projects throughout the region.

COAUTHOR

Erica Russell was reared in Oklahoma by her grandmother. She works in dentistry for more than fifteen years. She studies business administration at the renowned Oklahoma

City University. Erica also owns ELR Vending, a company that provides vending machines and services to Oklahoma businesses. She is passionate about increasing individuals' financial knowledge and status. She is a loyal leader in her church and devotes her time to equip other believers.

Income (after taxes)	Expected	Actual	Difference
Salary			
Spouses Salary			
Dividends			
Gifts			
Interest			
Investing Income			
Bonus			
Reimbursements			
Other			
Total			
Expenses	Expected	Actual	Difference
Mortgage/Rent			
Auto Loans			
Other Loans			
Auto Insurance			
Other Insurance			
Other Insurance			
Other Insurance			
Other Insurance			
Other Insurance			
Other Insurance			
Other Insurance			
Bank Charges			
Auto (fuel)			
Auto Maintenance			
Groceries			
Childcare			
Clothing			
Commuting Cost			

Electricity/Gas			
Water/Sewage			
Cable			
Entertainment			
Gifts Dispersed			
Cosmetics/Beauty			
Household Repairs			
Taxes			
Medical/Dental			
Other			
Total			
All Savings Total			
Income (after taxes)	Expected	Actual	Difference
Salary			
Spouses Salary			
Dividends			
Gifts			
Interest			
Investing Income			
Bonus			
Reimbursements			
Other			
Total			
Expenses	Expected	Actual	Difference
Mortgage/Rent			
Auto Loans			
Other Loans			
Auto Insurance			
Other Insurance			
Other Insurance			

Other Insurance			
Other Insurance			
Other Insurance			
Other Insurance			
Other Insurance			
Bank Charges			
Auto (fuel)			
Auto Maintenance			
Groceries			
Childcare			
Clothing			
Commuting Cost			
Electricity/Gas			
Water/Sewage			
Cable			
Entertainment			
Gifts Dispersed			
Cosmetics/Beauty			
Household Repairs			
Taxes			
Medical/Dental			
Other			
Total			
All Savings Total			
Income (after taxes)	Expected	Actual	Difference
Salary			
Spouses Salary			
Dividends			
Gifts			
Interest			

Investing Income			
Bonus			
Reimbursements			
Other			
Total			
Expenses	Expected	Actual	Difference
Mortgage/Rent			
Auto Loans			
Other Loans			
Auto Insurance			
Other Insurance			
Other Insurance			
Other Insurance			
Other Insurance			
Other Insurance			
Other Insurance			
Other Insurance			
Bank Charges			
Auto (fuel)			
Auto Maintenance			
Groceries			
Childcare			
Clothing			
Commuting Cost			
Electricity/Gas			
Water/Sewage			
Cable			
Entertainment			
Gifts Dispersed			
Cosmetics/Beauty			

Household Repairs			
Taxes			
Medical/Dental			
Other			
Total			
All Savings Total			
Income (after taxes)	Expected	Actual	Difference
Salary			
Spouses Salary			
Dividends			
Gifts			
Interest			
Investing Income			
Bonus			
Reimbursements			
Other			
Total			
Expenses	Expected	Actual	Difference
Mortgage/Rent			
Auto Loans			
Other Loans			
Auto Insurance			
Other Insurance			
Other Insurance			
Other Insurance			
Other Insurance			
Other Insurance			
Other Insurance			
Other Insurance			
Bank Charges			

Auto (fuel)			
Auto Maintenance			
Groceries			
Childcare			
Clothing			
Commuting Cost			
Electricity/Gas			
Water/Sewage			
Cable			
Entertainment			
Gifts Dispersed			
Cosmetics/Beauty			
Household Repairs			
Taxes			
Medical/Dental			
Other			
Total			
All Savings Total			
Income (after taxes)	Expected	Actual	Difference
Salary			
Spouses Salary			
Dividends			
Gifts			
Interest			
Investing Income			
Bonus			
Reimbursements			
Other			
Total			
Expenses	Expected	Actual	Difference

Mortgage/Rent			
Auto Loans			
Other Loans			
Auto Insurance			
Other Insurance			
Other Insurance			
Other Insurance			
Other Insurance			
Other Insurance			
Other Insurance			
Other Insurance			
Bank Charges			
Auto (fuel)			
Auto Maintenance			
Groceries			
Childcare			
Clothing			
Commuting Cost			
Electricity/Gas			
Water/Sewage			
Cable			
Entertainment			
Gifts Dispersed			
Cosmetics/Beauty			
Household Repairs			
Taxes			
Medical/Dental			
Other			
Total			
All Savings Total			

Income (after taxes)	Expected	Actual	Difference
Salary			
Spouses Salary			
Dividends			
Gifts			
Interest			
Investing Income			
Bonus			
Reimbursements			
Other			
Total			
Expenses	Expected	Actual	Difference
Mortgage/Rent			
Auto Loans			
Other Loans			
Auto Insurance			
Other Insurance			
Other Insurance			
Other Insurance			
Other Insurance			
Other Insurance			
Other Insurance			
Other Insurance			
Bank Charges			
Auto (fuel)			
Auto Maintenance			
Groceries			
Childcare			
Clothing			
Commuting Cost			

Electricity/Gas			
Water/Sewage			
Cable			
Entertainment			
Gifts Dispersed			
Cosmetics/Beauty			
Household Repairs			
Taxes			
Medical/Dental			
Other			
Total			
All Savings Total			